CHEATNOTES on LIFE
Lessons From The
Classroom Of Life

by Donna Blaurock

Cover Design by Julie Otlewis

Published By
Great Quotations
1967 Quincy Court
Glendale Heights, IL 60139

Printed in Hong Kong

Introduction

Upon graduating college, some are ready to conquer the world, while others are scared to death because they haven't a clue. This book has something for everyone. Filled with insight and sprinkled with inspiration, *Cheatnotes* will help bridge the gap between what is taught in school and what you *really* need to know in life beyond campus.

Many people have contributed their personal words of wisdom -- from business professionals to homemakers to some of life's greatest teachers. Their c*heatnotes* are simple, honest, enlightening and fun. And isn't that the way life ought to be?

As my grandfather would say, *just enjoy.*

Donna Blaurock

Look to this day, for it is life,
the very life of life. In its brief
course lie all the realities and verities
of existence; the bliss of growth, the splendor
of action, the glory of power. . .

For yesterday is but a dream, and tomorrow is only
a vision, but today, well lived, makes every
yesterday a dream of happiness and every
tomorrow a vision of hope.

— Sanskrit Proverb

Do what you WANT.
Not what you are *supposed* to do.

It is not enough to have an interesting or a good job. To live a total life, YOUR WORK MUST ALIGN WITH WHO YOU ARE.

STRESS or FUN?
It's your choice.

There is no such thing as a right or wrong decision — only THE decision.

You are not 'something.'
You are *SOMEONE*.

"Life is either a daring
adventure or nothing."

- Helen Keller

Be a TRAVELER of life;
not a tourist.

Upon dying, nobody ever said they
wished they had spent more time
at the office. Remember to
LIVE before you work.

Having children changes EVERYTHING.
Think about it for a few years.

BE ORIGINAL
Being anything else is *NOT*.

A professional looking resume
is important, but...

A RESUME DOES NOT
GET YOU A JOB.

If you can not BUDGET your
finances on $800 a month,
you'll have TROUBLE with
$8,000 a month.

Don't sell your *dreams* for $$$.

"The difference between a successful person
and others is not a lack of strength,
not a lack of knowledge,
but rather in a lack of will."

- Vincent Lombardi

Thirty or forty years in a career
is A LONG TIME. There is no rush.

ATTITUDE is more important than skills.
Fine-tune it.

Never put all your eggs in one basket.
Always have a safety net.

SAVE and INVEST as much as possible.
It is the oldest secret to becoming rich.

ENTRY LEVEL SALARIES ARE BELOW **POVERTY LEVEL**.

Don't work to improve someone else's business. Work to improve **YOURSELF**.

There will always be people who disagree. Stick to your guns and *avoid negative people*.

"Anybody can do anything.
It's just a matter of
believing in yourself."

- Motown Founder Berry Gordy

Rigid career planning may not work.
Keep an open mind and be flexible.

Focus on the present.
In dwelling on the past or living for
the future, you miss the moment.

APPLY FOR YOUR '**DREAM JOB**.'
With persistence, you just may get it.

FOCUS ON THREE YEAR GOALS.
Do not get bogged down by
'the rest of your life.'

If you worry about money,
you will have money worries.

BUY REPLACEMENT WARRANTIES.
More often than not, they
are worth every penny.

When it comes to religion,
don't follow. *FIND OUT.*

Even if you are on the right track,
you'll get run over if
you just sit there.

- Will Rogers

Others are mirrors of you.
Surround yourself with people
who reflect the BEST you.

Don't wait for flowers to be sent.
Plant your own garden.

Be appreciative of honest critics.
There's always room for improvement.

Don't worry about failure.
Worry about the chances you miss
when you don't even try.

Today, most people change careers
3 to 6 times over the course of their lives.

YOUR *1st* CAREER WILL NOT BE YOUR LAST.

When starting out, do not be so
concerned with *SALARY*.
Gaining experience and finding
what you enjoy is most important.

The ability to LISTEN will
help you in any industry.

If you quietly know what makes you
stand out from all others who do what you do,
and can communicate this clearly during
interviews with employers, you greatly
increase your chances of being the one chosen,
when there is a vacancy.

- Richard Bolles *What Color Is Your Parachute?*

It is still true — it's not what you know,
IT'S WHO YOU KNOW.
Be resourceful, join organizations and network.

Make a budget and strive to save
10% of your income.

JOB-HUNTING IS A FULL-TIME JOB.

EXPLORATION is as important as
the right direction. Take your time.

Regarding interviews,
do your homework:

RESEARCH THE ORGANIZATION.
DRESS PROFESSIONALLY.
BE CONFIDENT AND ENTHUSIASTIC.
ASK QUESTIONS.
SEND A THANK YOU.

"The secret of life
is enjoying the passage of time."

- James Taylor

How much you *TRUST* your mate is a good
indication of how secure the relationship is.

DON'T BURN ANY BRIDGES.
You never know when you'll need
family, friends and a good reference.

Read success stories for inspiration.
You'll find that there is no
ONE road to success and there is
no **ONE** definition for success.
It is simply a matter of opinion.

The surest way to get people to notice
you is to SMILE.

Try to remember the names of those you meet.
You will make a great 2nd impression.

"The only difference between a date and a job interview is that in not many job interviews is there a chance you'll wind up naked at the end of it."

- Jerry Seinfeld *SeinLanguage*

PAY CASH OR NOT AT ALL.
Use credit cards only for convenience.

PLAN AHEAD.
Open an I.R.A. (individual retirement account)
— tax-free, compounded interest does wonders.

VOTE.
It's your right.
It's your responsibility.

Don't allow the unimportant to
become important, nor the important
to become unimportant.

BE RESOURCEFUL.
If you don't know something, it usually takes
less than three phone calls.

Nature helps keep your spirit alive.
Watch the sun rise and set.
Listen to rain.
Gaze at stars.
Look for rainbows.
DON'T FORGET TO SMELL THE FLOWERS.

"Develop interest in life as you see it;
in people, things, literature, music
— the world is so rich, simply throbbing
with rich treasures, beautiful souls and
interesting people. Forget yourself."

- Henry Miller

OPEN YOUR HEART.
Let people in.

LOVE is not gazing into each other's eyes;
IT IS LOOKING TOGETHER
IN THE SAME DIRECTION.

TRUST YOUR INSTINCTS.
It has been said that your instincts
know long before your head has figured it out.

Eliminate 'SHOULD' from your vocabulary.

"You have brains in your head.
You have feet in your shoes.
You can steer yourself
any direction you choose."

- Dr. Seuss *Oh, The Places You'll Go!*

You can't take the weight of the world on your shoulders. *Don't even try.*

SHOW YOUR FEELINGS.
It takes too much energy not to.

LIFE is gained by living;
EXPERIENCE is gained by experiencing;
FRIENDS are gained by giving;
SKILL is gained by practicing;
KNOWLEDGE is gained by learning;
LOVE is gained by loving.

You have the power to
MAKE YOUR LIFE HAPPY.
Don't wait for someone or something.

Accept people for who they are.
TRYING TO CHANGE
SOMEONE DOESN'T WORK.

Make a list of everything you want in life.
REFER TO IT OFTEN.

Indecision gets you nowhere.
DON'T BE WISHY-WASHY.

"Pleasure is very seldom found
where it is sought; our brightest blazes
of gladness are commonly kindled
by unexpected sparks."

- Samual Johnson

Do not let the word 'NO' get in your way.
Every good salesman knows,
A SALE BEGINS WITH 'NO.'

DON'T IGNORE PROBLEMS.
Face them and they will no longer be problems.

Know all the ground rules from the start.
PUT EVERYTHING IN WRITING.

ADVERTISING SOMETIMES LIES.
Milk isn't that good for you.

Break unhealthy habits when you are young.
IF NOT NOW, WHEN?

Do not get *STUCK* in a job which is unsatisfying.
There is always something better
just around the corner.

"There is nothing greater in life
than loving another and being loved in return,
for loving is the ultimate of experiences."

- Leo Buscaglia

Don't expect to be taken care of.
Take the necessary steps to
SECURE YOUR FUTURE.

You can not know if a job suits you
until you are actually **IN IT**.

Never be miserable in a job or relationship.
Life is short. *MOVE ON.*

DON'T COMPARE OR CONFORM.
Give, be and do your very best.

ESTABLISH A MISSION
OR PURPOSE FOR YOUR LIFE.
Dedicate yourself to it.

Do not make MONEY your
primary motivation.

Believe that you can make positive change.
Then go out and PROVE IT.

Be as enthusiastic about the success
of *OTHERS* as you are of your own.

Gain solid work or volunteer experience
BEFORE deciding on graduate school.

"It's when you're safe at home that you
wish you were having an adventure.
When you're having an adventure
you wish you were safe at home."

- Thornton Wilder

Do not let job titles and
impressive salaries seduce you.
LOOK BEYOND THE GLITTER.

If you think you are educated now,
YOU'VE GOT A LOT TO LEARN.

"If one advances confidently, in the direction
of his own dreams and endeavors,
to lead the life which he has imagined,
he will meet with a success
unexpected in common hours."

- Henry David Thoreau

Look for the GOOD in people.
Find ways to make them feel SPECIAL.

Have some sort of support system.
Surround yourself with *LIKE-MINDED* people.

There is a purpose for you being here.
DISCOVER what that is and PURSUE IT.

If you are considering investing in a
small business, consider this:
75% percent FAIL within 5 to 6 years.

FIND A MENTOR OR ROLE MODEL —
somebody you have a rapport with
and a respect for, preferably in your
chosen career field.

The difference between ordinary and
extraordinary is that **LITTLE EXTRA**.

"The time to repair the roof
is when the sun is shining."

- John F. Kennedy

Have lots of relationships when you are young.
DO NOT HURRY UP and *SETTLE DOWN*.

Practice safe sex. DON'T GAMBLE.
Sooner or later, you lose.

Be adventurous and courageous —
TAKE THE ROAD LESS TRAVELED.

There are no mistakes; only lessons.
As long as you are alive,
THE LESSONS DO NOT END.

CARPE DIEM.
Seize every opportunity.

"Never try to take the manners of another
as your own, for the theft will be immediately
evident and the thief will appear as
ridiculous as a robin with
peacock feathers hastily stuck on."

- Maya Angelou   *Wouldn't Take Nothing For My Journey Now*

STICK WITH PEOPLE WHO
MAKE YOU LAUGH.
They are much less expensive
than a therapist.

Timing is everything.
When you are ready, *IT* will happen.

TAKE TO THE WORLD AND LEARN.
Sit in a cafe and talk to some rednecks;
take a train across India;
walk the continental divide —
go somplace and be uncomfortable for awhile.
Feel the ugly and the beauty of the world.

Beware of anything RICH.
There is such a thing as overdoing it.

DON'T BLAME.
You are responsible for your life.

KEEP YOUR PERSPECTIVE.
Even the worst jobs
are good experience.

Life is full of choices.
CHOOSE LOVE.

Have your PRIORITIES straight.
Don't take HEALTH, FAMILY or
a ROOF OVER YOUR HEAD for granted.

If what you are doing is not moving you
toward your goals, it is moving you
away from your goals.

- Brian Tracy

BUYING RETAIL IS STUPID.
Whenever possible, cut out the middleman.

Do not forget how to USE THE LIBRARY.
But if you do, ASK a reference librarian.

Investigate your options.
DON'T JUST SETTLE for the
conventional career path.
THERE ARE ALTERNATIVES.

Consider taking 'TIME OUT' to work,
or volunteer abroad. The rewards are infinitely
greater than a job at home.

The success rate of partnerships in
business is not much better than marriages.
THINK TWICE BEFORE MIXING
BUSINESS WITH FRIENDSHIP.

A good computer is worth the investment.

Make sure the person you marry
feels the same as you do regarding life goals,
money, children and religion.

Don't wait for 'mid-life' to
begin soul searching.
RE-EVALUATE NOW and continue
to do so every few years.

"Work is something connected to the self,
a part of the spirit, mind, body and senses —
a mirror of the person."

- Marsha Sinetar *Do What You Love, The Money Will Follow*

DON'T TRY TO GROW UP TOO FAST.
Being an adult lasts a long time in
relation to your teens and early 20's.

Do SOMETHING to make this planet a
better place for you having been here.

Internships and volunteer work are
GREAT OPPORTUNITIES to
test the waters for future careers.
They also look good on a resume.

The fantasy of 'wanting out' of the rat race
is very common. Ask yourself, WHY?

Do not let peers or others
influence your decisions.
Take advice with a grain of salt
and FOLLOW YOUR GUT.

Read all kinds of different books —
they are full of *CHEATNOTES*.

STRETCH BEYOND YOUR *COMFORT ZONE*
and your perception of the world
will be a lot larger than you can imagine now.

Today, there is NO SUCH THING
AS JOB SECURITY.
You've got to look beyond the
job market and search within yourself.

Learn to FORGIVE.
Everyone makes mistakes.

FEAR AND DREAMS DON'T MIX.
Do not allow fears to override passions.

"I believe this now without question.
Income, position, the opinion of one's peers
and all the other traditional criteria
by which human beings are
generally judged are for the birds."

- James A. Michener

BE INDEPENDENT.
Do not follow where the path may lead.
Go instead where there is
no path and leave a trail.

Maturity is not a matter of age.
It comes with *UNDERSTANDING*.

THE EXPLORER, not the
mountain climber,
is the one likely to discover
a better place to dwell.

When it comes to travel, the more money
you spend, the LESS you experience.

Work needs to *FIT* your personality just
as a shoe needs to fit your feet.

Don't take marriage LIGHTLY.

TAKE RISKS. You cannot discover
new oceans unless you have the courage
to lose sight of the shore.

Most genius is MULTIFACETED.
Even Einstein loved music as
much as he loved physics.

Every great novelist, salesman,
doctor or performer began as an
INEXPERIENCED BEGINNER.

We make a living by what we get,
but we make a life by what we give.

- Winston Churchill

When one door closes,
ANOTHER ONE OPENS.

There are some things you MUST do
while you are young and/or in shape,
like hiking the Grand Canyon
or running a marathon.

Nothing is really work unless you would rather be doing **SOMETHING ELSE.**

Sometimes, there's no way to find out whether or not a particular path really suits you except by trying it. Even if it doesn't, you will have gained something PRICELESS.

UNDERSTANDING is one thing
and ACTION is another.
You can spend years understanding your fear
of water and still never walk to the edge
of the pool and jump in.

THE ONLY PERSON YOU HAVE
TO SATISFY IS YOURSELF.

"The secret of happiness is not found
in seeking more, but in developing
the capacity to enjoy less."

- Dan Millman, *Way of the Peaceful Warrior*

LEARN TO TYPE.
Employment agencies don't care
what college you attended;
they want to know how fast you can type.

The world outside of campus is INFLEXIBLE.
You will have to conform to other
people's schedules for everything
including when you eat lunch.

FORGET ABOUT SUMMER VACATION.
In the real world, you get
TWO WEEKS vacation a year.

Read business, financial and
trade publications to
STAY ABREAST OF CURRENT TRENDS.

SUCCESS is a journey — not a destination.
Half the fun is getting there. **ENJOY THE RIDE.**

For every person, there is another
person that matches.
Until you meet, you'll never be COMPLETE.

COMMENCEMENT does not
just mean graduation —
it means A NEW BEGINNING.

DIETS DON'T WORK. They make you hungry.
Don't get caught in the yo-yo syndrome.
Develop good eating habits NOW.

VISIT YOUR DENTIST at least once a year.
PREVENTION is cheaper than root canals.

"If you are only making a living at what you do,
going into work because it is a job,
it won't take very long before you'll feel
empty inside and lack purpose in your life."

- Dr. Wayne Dyer *The Sky's The Limit*

MONEY IS FREEDOM.
Freedom is the ability to do what you
want to do when you want to do it.

If you are not part of the SOLUTION,
you are part of the PROBLEM.

SEEK PROGRESS; not perfection.

Don't sleep your life away.
Get out of bed EARLY even if you
are temporarily unemployed.

If you associate work with stress,
drudgery, regimentation and confinement,
it may be TIME FOR A CHANGE.

The one who loves the least
CONTROLS the relationship.

The biggest risk in life
is NOT RISKING.

The way to win is to make it OKAY to lose.

"Life is about opening yourself
up to possibilities.
That's what life is about."

- Oprah Winfrey

If you want to become a better writer,
KEEP WRITING.

Failures are just STEPPING STONES
to success in disguise.
Sometimes you need to fail
in order to succeed.

If you have a college degree you
can be sure of one thing...
YOU HAVE A COLLEGE DEGREE.

Your parents are not your enemy.
Do what you must to MAKE PEACE with them
and COMMUNICATE.

The *SECRET* of all genuinely successful people
is that they have found their paths.

"The real voyage of discovery consists not
in seeking new landscapes,
but in having new eyes."

- Marcel Proust

NOBODY MAKES IT ON THEIR OWN.
Don't be afraid to ask for help or advice.

Obstacles like money, habit, fear and
other people can all be overcome.
NOTHING CAN STOP YOU
when you are moving in the
direction of your dreams.

Money is only complicated if you
make it complicated.
If you can live modestly and
manage your money wisely,
YOU REALLY DON'T NEED THAT MUCH.

YOU ARE NEVER TOO OLD TO
HAVE A HAPPY CHILDHOOD.

Reading all the 'success' books
in the world will not give you the recipe
YOU need for success.
IT'S UP TO YOU TO WRITE
YOUR OWN SUCCESS STORY.

If you feel you are in the wrong job
or you are in a job in which you
are under-employed, you probably are.
CONTINUE LOOKING.

"You gotta be hungry."

- Les Brown *Live Your Dreams*

The average job in this country
only lasts about 3.6 years.

To be hired for a position, you must
SHOW AN EMPLOYER HOW YOUR
SKILLS WILL HELP THEM WITH
THEIR PROBLEMS AND INCREASE PROFITS.

Whenever possible, AVOID LAWSUITS.
The only ones who win are the lawyers.

NEVER RELY on roommates to
pay a bill that is in your name.
It could ruin your credit.

Whatever you do,
DON'T WAIT FOR RETIREMENT
TO START TRAVELING.

College graduates are a dime a dozen today.
You must make yourself STAND OUT.

DON'T PROCRASTINATE.
Put goals in writing where
you can see them daily.

When leaving a job,
ASK FOR A LETTER OF RECOMMENDATION.

INVESTIGATE STRATEGIES
to reduce your taxes or make deductions.

"By working hard eight hours a day,
you may eventually get to be boss
and work hard twelve hours a day."

- Robert Frost

BE PREPARED.
Carry jumper cables in your car.
Have your license, auto club card
and insurance card handy.

Don't wait for a red light to go on
before checking the oil in your car.
Make it a HABIT to check the oil,
tires and water periodically.

LEARN ABOUT INVESTING in
mutual funds and stocks.
Read and ask questions.

FIND A BALANCE between
business and pleasure.

Save old notes and letters from
high school and college.
Someday, you will laugh
at how SERIOUS it all seemed.

Pay your bills and taxes ON TIME.

Companies don't succeed...
PEOPLE do.

HAVE PATIENCE.
Anything worth having is worth waiting for.

When you exaggerate,
you WEAKEN your story.

Shoes and belts say a lot
about a person's *STYLE*.

Some people are not cut out for
the corporate culture.
If you can't stand the heat,
GET OUT OF THE KITCHEN.

SAVE ALL RECEIPTS.

Make a spare copy of important keys
and REMEMBER WHERE YOU PUT THEM.

"How you feel is not the result of
what is happening in your life —
it is your *interpretation* of what is happening."

- Anthony Robbins *Unlimited Power*

There are times to play it safe
and not take chances.
REFUSE TO GET IN A CAR WITH ANYONE
WHO HAS BEEN DRINKING.

Parents mean well, but they don't
ALWAYS know best.

A wealthy person is not necessarily
a SUCCESSFUL person.
Don't confuse the two.

QUALITY IS NEVER AN ACCIDENT.
It is always the result of high intention,
sincere effort, intelligent direction
and skillfull execution.

If you don't take care
of your customers,
SOMEBODY ELSE WILL.

Purchase a daily planner and
carry it with you everywhere you go.

When it comes to matters of importance,
WRITE THEM DOWN to be safe.

You've got to EAT. You've got to BREATHE.
And you've got to MOVE.

- Susan Powter *Stop The Insanity*

Consider living together before marriage.
You can not really *KNOW* someone
until you live with them.

If you think you have a great idea,
DON'T LET ANYONE TALK YOU OUT OF IT
even if it sounds foolish.
Remember the pet rock.

When seeking career advice
or medical opinions,
consult at least *THREE* sources.

BE CAREFUL what you say around children.
They will listen and repeat EVERYTHING.

Words are words.
The best teachers are those who
SET AN EXAMPLE.

DO SOMETHING CHARITABLE.
Give what you can, be it time
or money, to a good cause.

BE REALISTIC.
You may have to start
in the mailroom.

MANY ARTISTS CREATED THEIR
MOST FAMOUS WORKS IN THE 20'S.
Michelangelo's 'David' and Einstein's
theory of relativity were both fashioned
when their creators were twenty-six.

There is nothing to be ashamed of if you
change your mind. *REMAIN FLEXIBLE.*

'Sidejobs' are a great way to earn extra income.
Make up a flyer and
MARKET YOUR TIME OR SKILLS.

If a particular career sounds intriguing,
ask someone what it is
they actually *DO* all day.

The average time after graduation
before a liberal arts major finds a job
in a career area of choice is
between eight and ten months.

Setting goals is easy.
STICKING TO THEM is the tough part.

"The art of getting rich is found not in saving,
but in being at the right spot at the right time."

- Ralph Waldo Emerson   *The Conduct of Life*

PRACTICE WHAT YOU PREACH.
Work for a company who does the same.

Don't take a job out of DESPERATION.
It's better to work part-time and continue
to look for what you really want.

ALWAYS BE THE 'REAL YOU.'

Keep your personal life and
your work life SEPARATE.

If you experience 'reality shock'
on your first job, know that
YOU ARE NOT ALONE.

Most new jobs (about two thirds)
are in SMALL business.
Ninety percent are in SERVICE industries.

YOU MUST BE TRAINABLE.
Keep a positive attitude toward
instruction and training.

If you are in your early 20s,
statistically you have approximately
60 MORE YEARS on planet Earth.

"Education is what you learn after
you have forgotten everything
you learned in school."

- Abert Einstein

Anything which sounds
'too good to be true' USUALLY IS.

If you are thinking of starting
your own small business,
count on needing at least 50 percent MORE
capital than you originally anticipated.

You can be OLD at age 30
or YOUNG at age 70.
IT'S ALL A STATE OF MIND.

Take time for yourself everyday to
do something JUST FOR YOU.

PRINCES SOMETIMES TURN BACK INTO FROGS.

Children grow up but they don't go away.
Have them if you are willing to SACRIFICE.

Success is 50% what you know and 50%
how you COMMUNICATE what you know.

POSTPONE BUYING THE
NEW BMW FOR AWHILE.

HAVE A RAINY DAY FUND that you
can survive on should you be
out of work for six months.

When you are young and in good health,
purchase only major medical health insurance
with a $1,000 - $2,500 deductible.

CHANGE is the only GUARANTEE
for the future.

LEARN TO COOK.
You'd be amazed at how much you
can save just by eating at home
instead of going out.

"Nothing is as real as a dream.
And if you go for it, something really good
is going to happen to you.
You may grow old,
but you never really get old."

- Tom Clancy

When buying a car, don't just be
concerned about the *PRICE*.
Find out how much it costs to INSURE it.
That can be the REAL KILLER in the long run.

Try NEW things. Taste NEW foods.
Have NEW experiences.

"If you are single with no dependents,
don't buy life insurance.
Invest your money for use
while you are young."

- Charles J. Givens *Wealth Without Risk*

Employers don't want excuses.
They want **RESULTS.**

Communication skills are vital.
Speak and write with
CLARITY, SINCERITY AND BREVITY.

YOU ARE WHAT YOU *THINK* YOU ARE.

"Adults don't ask questions as a child does.
When you stop wondering, you might as well
put your rocker on the
front porch and call it a day."

- Johnny Carson

LIFE IS ABOUT LEARNING LESSONS.
A lesson will be presented to you in
various forms until you have learned it.
When you have learned it, you can then
go on to the next lesson.

Your greatest asset is
YOUR INDIVIDUALITY.
Express it.

Don't accept advice from
anyone who doesn't have
his own act together.

Remember the rule of MODERATION.
Even sunshine burns if you get too much.

Do not let anyone tell you that your
experience is not 'reality.'
YOUR EXPERIENCE IS YOUR REALITY.

The first step in discovering your path is to
IDENTIFY THE THINGS THAT
LIGHT YOU FROM WITHIN.

Resources like books, pamphlets, magazines,
organizations, people, networks,
newsletters and counseling services will
lead you to a thousand other resources.

"From now until the year 2005,
the number of college graduates will
outpace the number of available jobs
by 20% each year."

- U.S. Labor Department, 1993

ALUMNI are great sources
for jobs or job leads.

Corporate recruiters overwhelmingly specify
LEADERSHIP and INTERPERSONAL SKILLS
as the assets they seek
in managerial candidates.

When people say it isn't the money,
it's the principle, you can be sure
IT'S THE MONEY.

A simple time management strategy:
HAVE A SYSTEM. STICK TO IT.
WRITE EVERYTHING DOWN.